Bizarre Beast Battles
HIPPO VS. POLAR BEAR
I0797582
Gareth Stevens
PUBLISHING
By Janey Levy

Please visit our website, www.garethstevens.com. For a free color catalog of all our high-quality books, call toll free 1-800-542-2595 or fax 1-877-542-2596.

Cataloging-in-Publication Data

Names: Levy, Janey.
Title: Hippo vs. polar bear / Janey Levy.
Description: New York : Gareth Stevens Publishing, 2019. | Series: Bizarre beast battles | Includes glossary and index.
Identifiers: LCCN ISBN 9781538219294 (pbk.) | ISBN 9781538219270 (library bound) | ISBN 9781538219300 (6 pack)
Subjects: LCSH: Hippopotamus–Juvenile literature. | Polar bear–Juvenile literature.
Classification: LCC QL737.U57 L48 2019 | DDC 599.63'5–dc23

First Edition

Published in 2019 by
Gareth Stevens Publishing
111 East 14th Street, Suite 349
New York, NY 10003

Designer: Katelyn E. Reynolds
Editor: Monika Davies

Photo credits: Cover, p. 1 (hippo) Fuse/Corbis/Getty Images; cover, p. 1 (polar bear) jeryltan/E+/Getty Images; cover, pp. 1–24 (background texture) Apostrophe/Shutterstock.com; pp. 4–21 (hippo icon) Miceking/Shutterstock.com; pp. 4–21 (polar bear icon) KATE_123/Shutterstock.com; p. 5 Karel Bartik/Shutterstock.com; p. 7 John Shaw/Science Source/Getty Images; p. 8 JMx Images/Shutterstock.com; p. 9 Vaclav Sebek/Shutterstock.com; p. 10 Digital Vision./DigitalVision/Getty Images; p. 11 (main) Nirut Sampan/Shutterstock.com; p. 11 (inset) Nagel Photography/Shutterstock.com; p. 12 Vaclav Silha/Barcroft USA/Getty Images; p. 13 Paul Souders/Corbis Documentary/Getty Images; p. 14 MARK RALSTON/AFP/Getty Images; p. 15 spxChrome/E+/Getty Images; p. 16 Johan Swanepoel/Shutterstock.com; p. 17 critterbiz/Shutterstock.com; p. 18 Ondrej Prosicky/Shutterstock.com; p. 19 La Nau de Fotografia/Shutterstock.com; p. 21 (hippo) Dennis Stewrt/Shutterstock.com; p. 21 (polar bear) Robert Sarosiek/Shutterstock.com.

Printed in the United States of America

CPSIA compliance information: Batch #CS18GS: For further information contact Gareth Stevens, New York, New York at 1-800-542-2595.

CONTENTS

Words in the glossary appear in **bold** type the first time they are used in the text.

HUMONGOUS HIPPOS

Hippos are huge **mammals** that live in eastern, central, and southern Africa. They have a large, round body and short, fat legs. Their broad mouth can open very wide.

Hippos spend their days in water and come onto land at night to eat. They're herbivores, or plant eaters, which doesn't sound scary. But hippos are among the most feared animals in Africa. They're territorial, **aggressive**, and sometimes fight for **mates**. Their large size makes them dangerous, and their giant mouth holds some sharp teeth.

"Hippopotamus" means "river horse" in Greek. But hippos aren't really **related** to horses. Their closest living relatives are likely whales and dolphins!

PREDATORY POLAR BEARS

Polar bears live throughout the Arctic. They have a large, heavy body with strong legs and a long neck. Their huge paws have sharp claws. Sharp teeth fill the mouth in their narrow head. They're perfectly built for traveling on ice and swimming in cold waters.

Polar bears are the largest land carnivores, or meat eaters, in the world. They aren't territorial and have no natural predators. But their claws and teeth are **weapons** as they hunt **prey** and fight for mates.

Polar bears are also known as ice bears, sea bears, and white bears.

POUND FOR POUND

Hippos and polar bears are both dangerous animals. But they live in completely different **habitats**. Hippos live in warm places in Africa, while polar bears live in the cold, icy Arctic. Let's see how these two scary mammals match up!

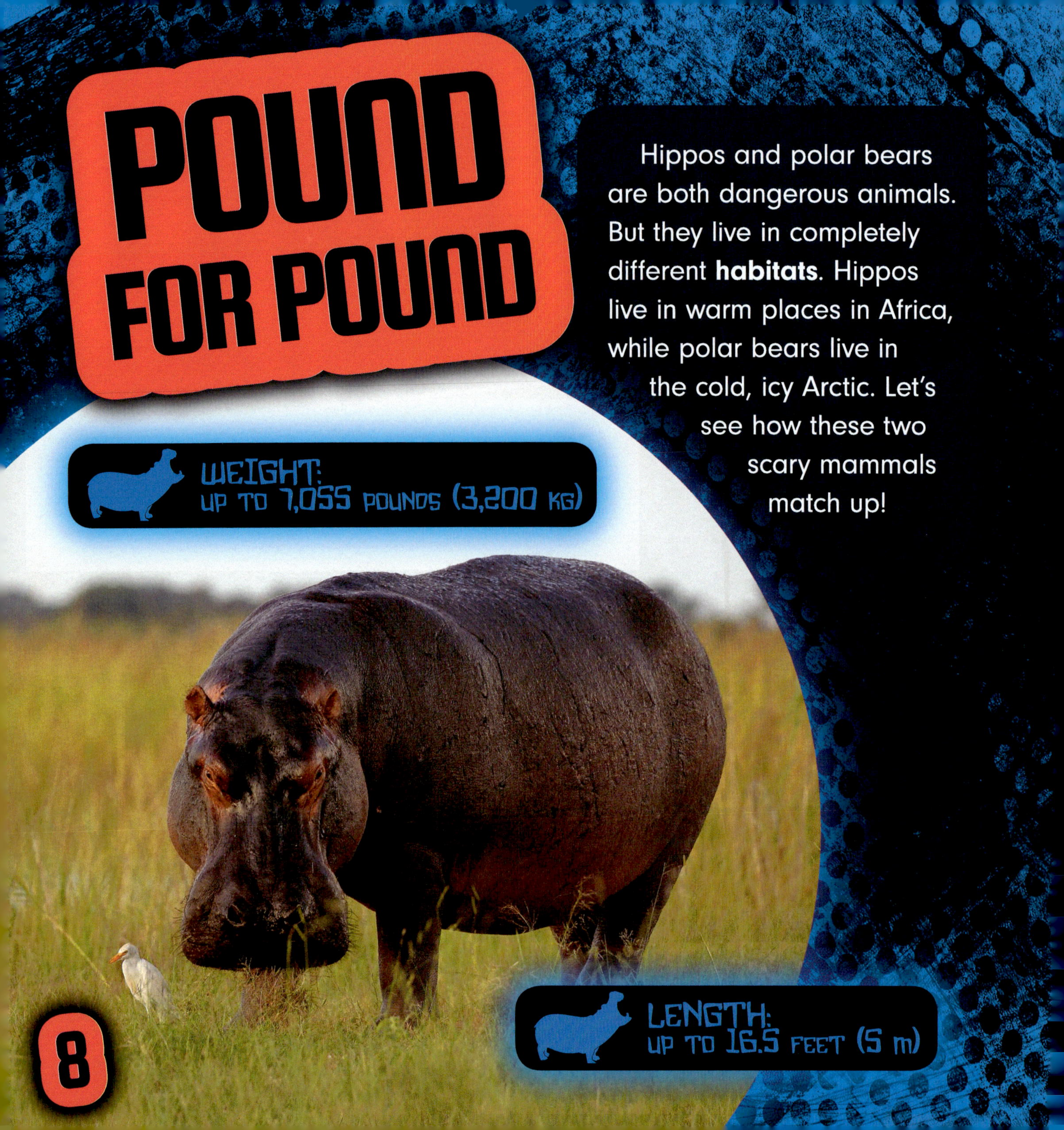

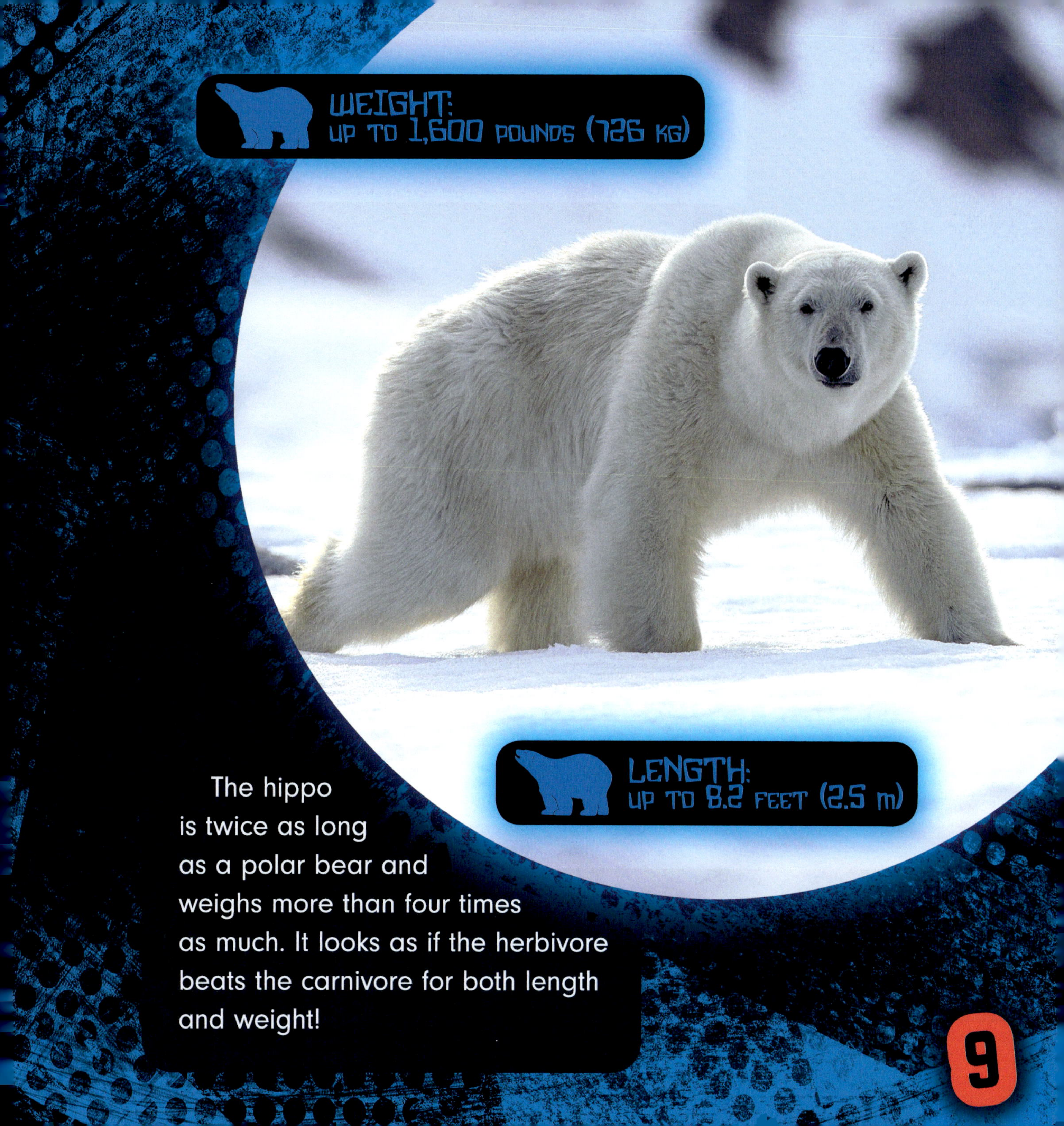

The hippo is twice as long as a polar bear and weighs more than four times as much. It looks as if the herbivore beats the carnivore for both length and weight!

TOOTH AND CLAW

Hippos have 36 teeth. Their back teeth are flat for chewing food. But in front, they have long, sharp teeth called **canines** for fighting.

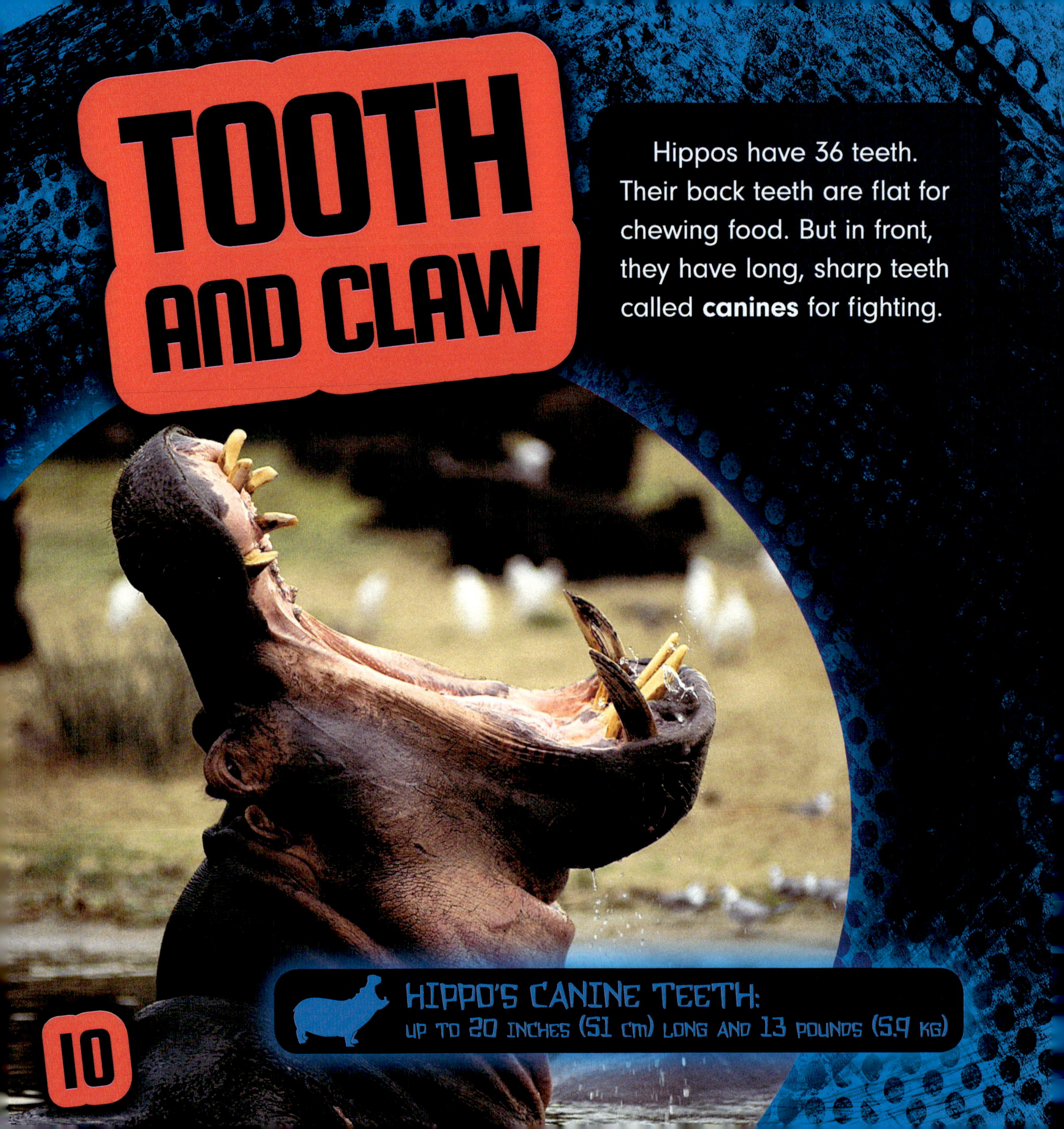

HIPPO'S CANINE TEETH:
UP TO 20 INCHES (51 CM) LONG AND 13 POUNDS (5.9 KG)

Polar bears have 42 jagged, or uneven, teeth and strong, curved claws. Both serve them well as they hunt prey and fight for mates.

The polar bear has more teeth, all of which are sharp, and it has claws, too. But a hippo's canine teeth are much longer and heavier. This might be a draw!

BITE DOWN

In addition to their frightening teeth, hippos have powerful bites. A hippo's bite can squash a crocodile or break a boat!

HIPPO'S BITE FORCE:
1,800 POUNDS PER SQUARE INCH

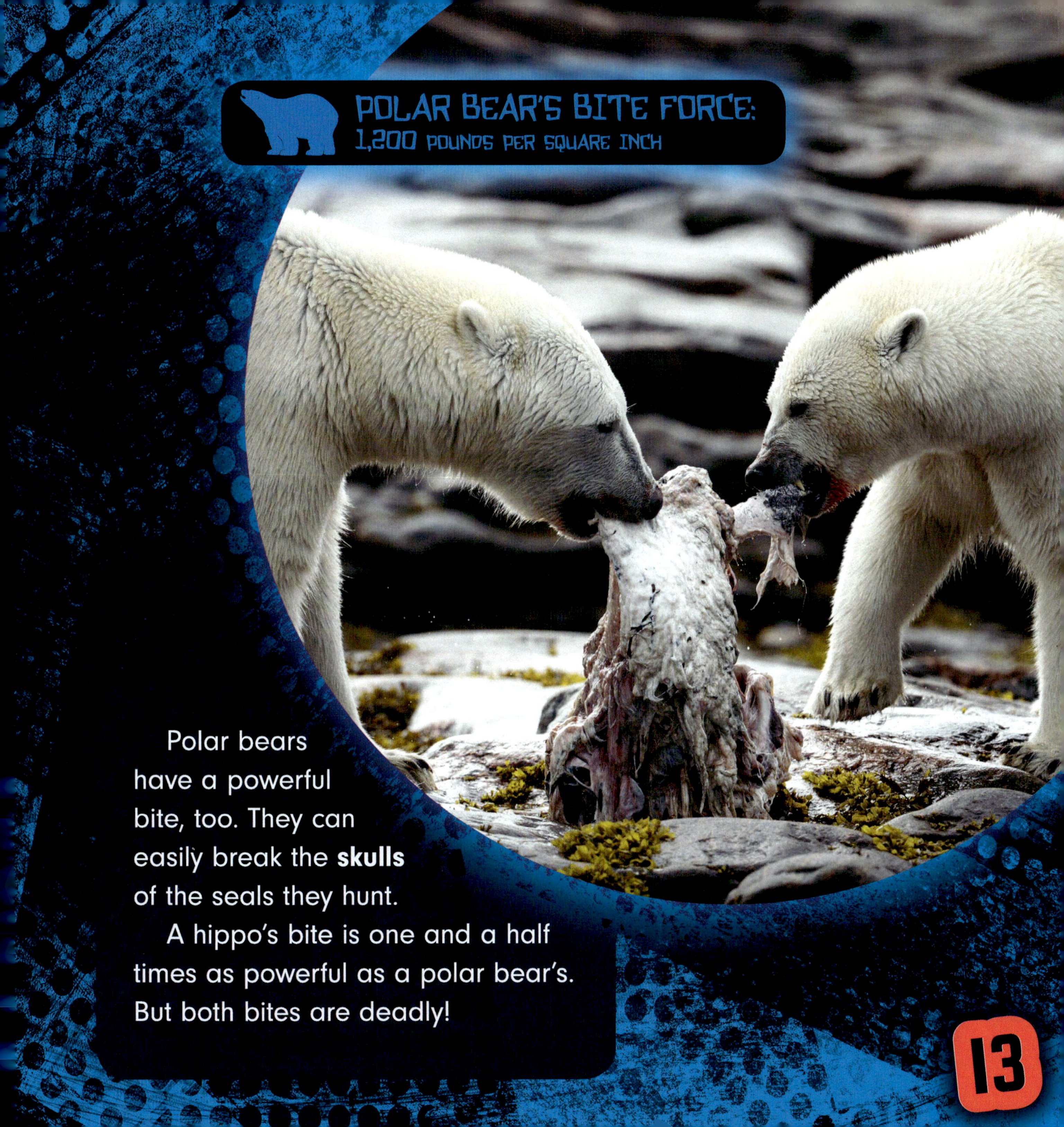

POLAR BEAR'S BITE FORCE:
1,200 POUNDS PER SQUARE INCH

Polar bears have a powerful bite, too. They can easily break the **skulls** of the seals they hunt.

A hippo's bite is one and a half times as powerful as a polar bear's. But both bites are deadly!

TOP SPEED

For such big, heavy animals, hippos can move surprisingly fast. They can outrun the world's fastest human! In water, they can move almost as fast as a prize-winning swimmer.

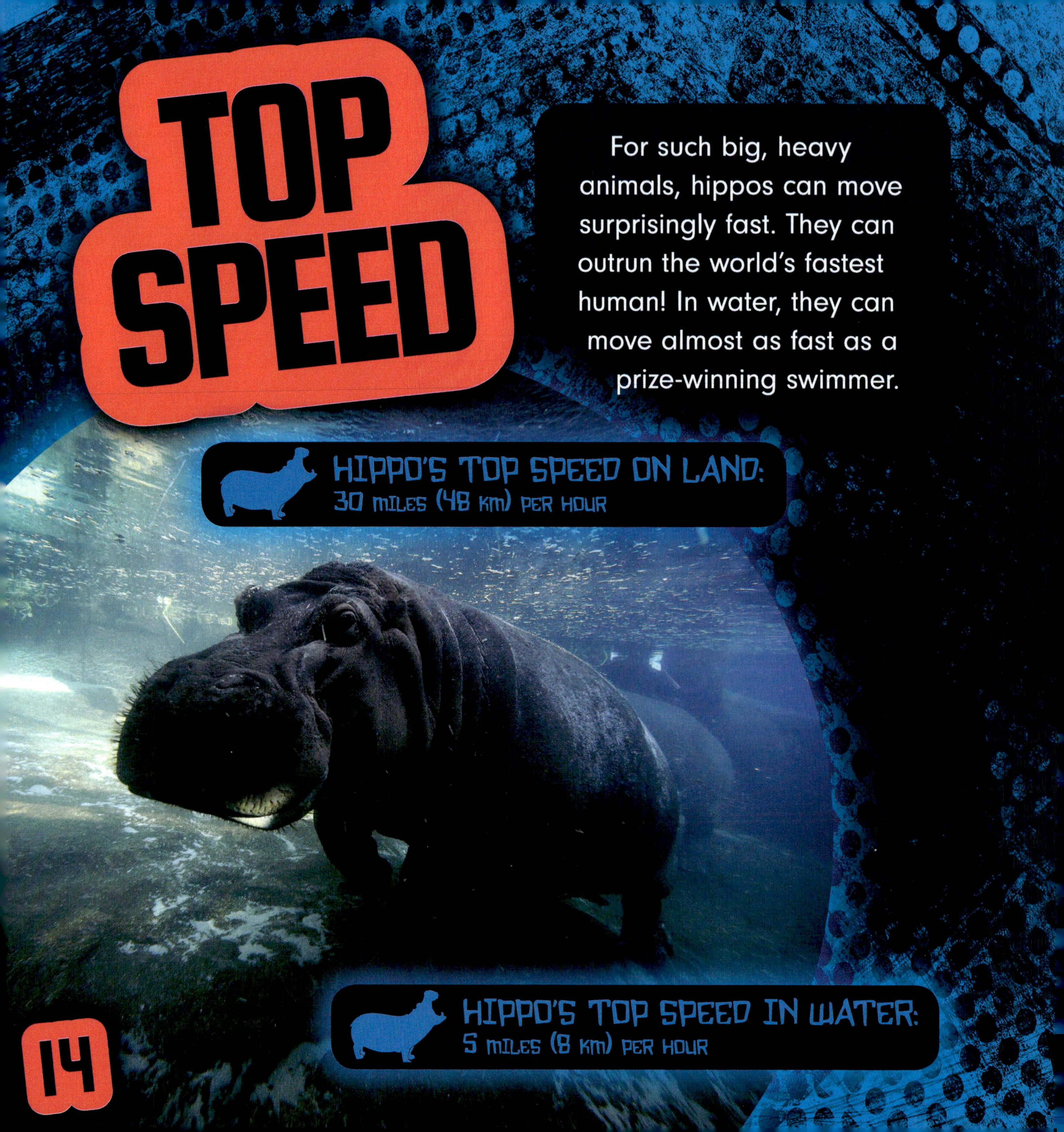

HIPPO'S TOP SPEED ON LAND:
30 MILES (48 KM) PER HOUR

HIPPO'S TOP SPEED IN WATER:
5 MILES (8 KM) PER HOUR

POLAR BEAR'S TOP SPEED IN WATER:
6 MILES (9.7 KM) PER HOUR

Polar bears are also quick runners. Their swimming speed equals that of the fastest human swimmer.

Hippos win the race on land, but polar bears win in the water. However, they'd both beat you!

POLAR BEAR'S TOP SPEED ON LAND:
25 MILES (40 KM) PER HOUR

BITTER BATTLES

Male hippos fight each other for territory and the right to mate with females. They use their sharp teeth and huge, heavy head as weapons. Hippos sometimes die in these battles.

ATTACK METHODS OF A HIPPO:

- ROARS, HONKS, AND **SNORTS** TO SCARE OFF THEIR **RIVAL**
- OPENS MOUTH WIDE TO SHOW OFF THEIR CANINES
- BITES THEIR RIVAL'S TAIL, LEGS, AND BODY
- USES HEAD LIKE A HAMMER

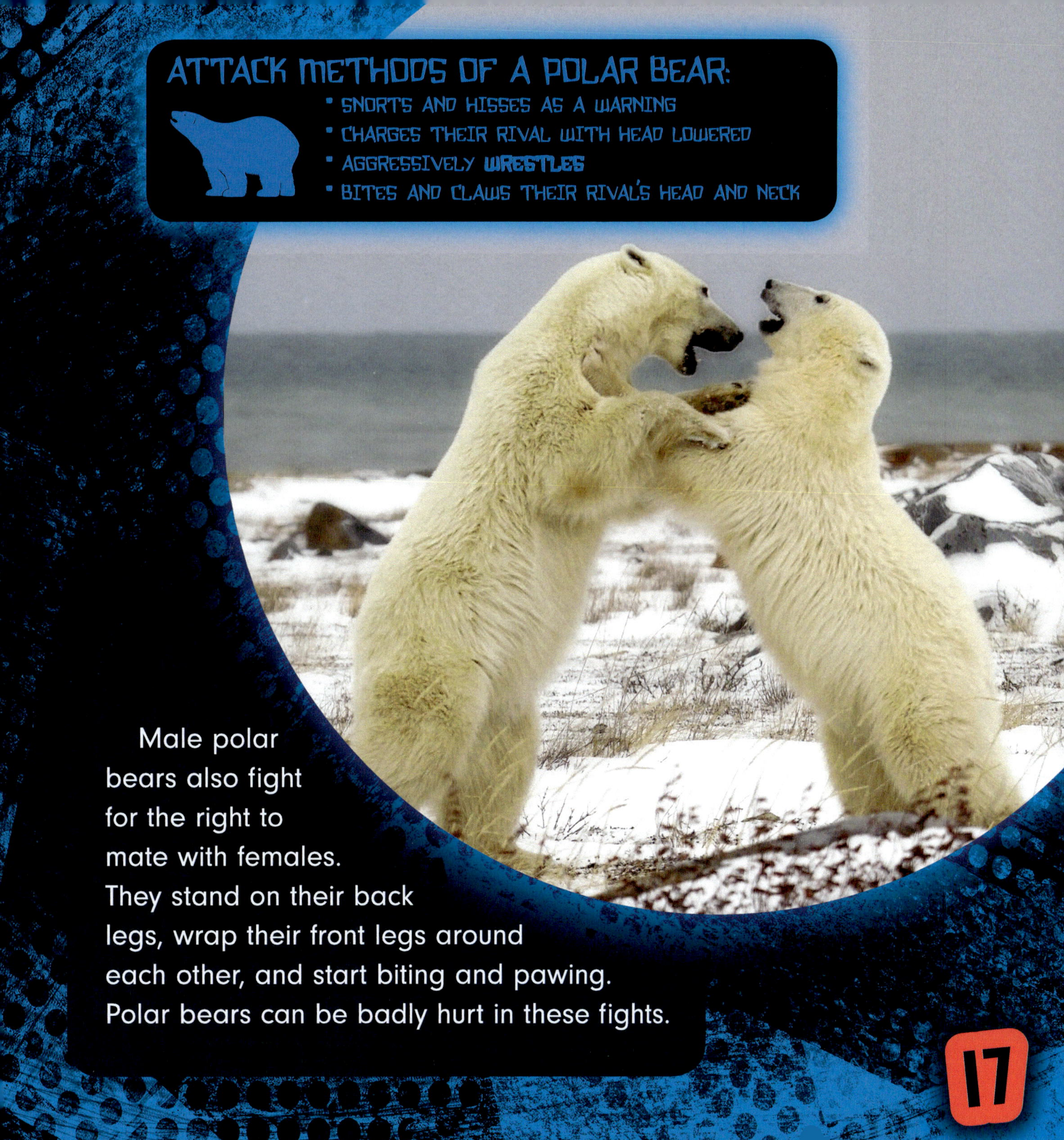

ATTACK METHODS OF A POLAR BEAR:

- SNORTS AND HISSES AS A WARNING
- CHARGES THEIR RIVAL WITH HEAD LOWERED
- AGGRESSIVELY **WRESTLES**
- BITES AND CLAWS THEIR RIVAL'S HEAD AND NECK

Male polar bears also fight for the right to mate with females. They stand on their back legs, wrap their front legs around each other, and start biting and pawing. Polar bears can be badly hurt in these fights.

LIFE-SPAN

Even though male hippos can die in their fights, most hippos have a long **life-span**. That's because they have few predators. The biggest danger to them comes from people, who have harmed and reduced their habitat.

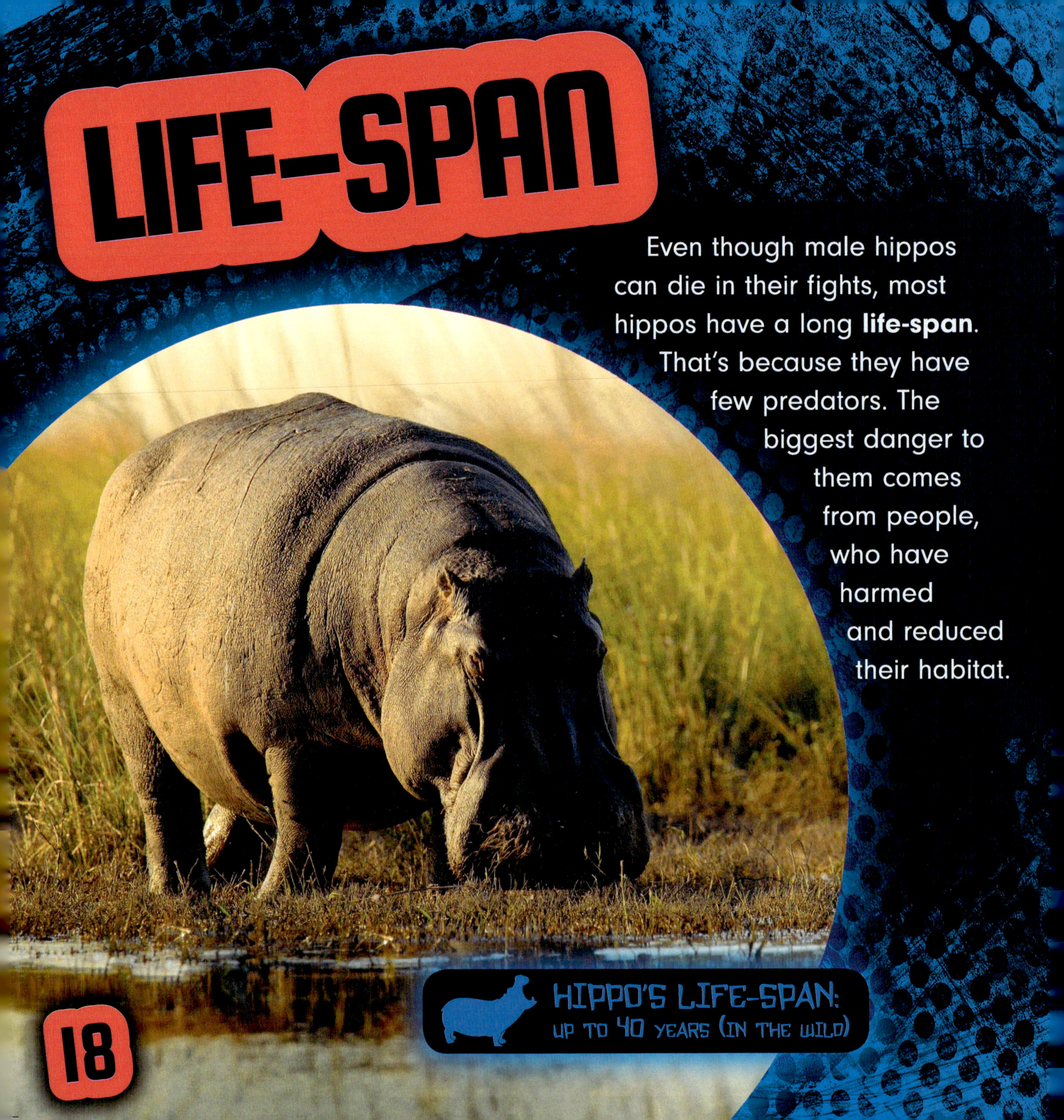

HIPPO'S LIFE-SPAN:
UP TO 40 YEARS (IN THE WILD)

POLAR BEAR'S LIFE-SPAN:
25 TO 30 YEARS (IN THE WILD)

Life in the polar bears' Arctic habitat is hard. Still, polar bears are able to live long lives. Yet hippos can live much longer. Hippos are the winners here!

WHO'S THE WINNER?

Now that you know more about these two mammals, who do you think would win if they battled to the death? The hippo is larger, but the polar bear has claws and a greater number of sharp teeth. However, the hippo has a more powerful bite.

It seems the hippo wins in most areas. But the polar bear is a carnivore and hunter, while the hippo is a herbivore. Does that give the polar bear a winning advantage? You decide!

BECAUSE THE HIPPO AND THE POLAR BEAR LIVE IN COMPLETELY DIFFERENT PARTS OF THE WORLD, THEY WOULD NEVER ACTUALLY MEET. SO, THIS BIZARRE BEAST BATTLE IS IMPOSSIBLE. BUT IT'S FUN TO IMAGINE!

GLOSSARY

aggressive: showing a readiness to attack

canine: a long, pointed tooth near the front of the mouth

habitat: the natural place where an animal or plant lives

life-span: how long a person or animal lives

mammal: a warm-blooded animal that has a backbone and hair, breathes air, and feeds milk to its young

mate: one of two animals that come together to produce babies; to come together to make babies

prey: an animal that is hunted by other animals for food

rival: an animal or person who tries to be more successful than another

related: two people or animals connected by family

skull: the boney frame of the head and face

snort: the act or sound of loudly forcing air through the nose

weapon: something used to fight an enemy

wrestle: to fight by gripping, holding, and pushing rather than hitting

FOR MORE INFORMATION

BOOKS

Gregory, Josh. *Hippopotamuses.* New York, NY: Children's Press, 2017.

Newman, Mark. *Polar Bears.* New York, NY: Square Fish, 2015.

Owings, Lisa. *The Polar Bear.* Minneapolis, MN: Bellwether Media, 2013.

WEBSITES

10 Hippo Facts!
www.natgeokids.com/nz/discover/animals/general-animals/ten-hippo-facts/
Visit this site to learn more about hippos.

21 Cool Polar Bear Facts
zoonooz.sandiegozoo.org/2015/12/06/21-cool-polar-bear-facts/
Dive into the cool world of polar bears with this list of fun facts from the San Diego Zoo!

Publisher's note to educators and parents: Our editors have carefully reviewed these websites to ensure that they are suitable for students. Many websites change frequently, however, and we cannot guarantee that a site's future contents will continue to meet our high standards of quality and educational value. Be advised that students should be closely supervised whenever they access the internet.

INDEX